BRAIN WAVES

POETRY

Chris Webster

Contents

© 1990 Folens Limited, on behalf of the author.

Illustration by Linda Robson. Cover design by Robert J. Gee.
Our thanks to Noreen Lomasney for all her help.
First published 1990 by Folens Limited, Dunstable and Dublin.

ISBN 185276 063X

Folens Limited. Apex Business Centre, Boscombe Road, Dunstable LU5 4RL, England.

Poetry in the National Curriculum.

Sita and Mark are working on the *Best Words* sheet. Listen to their conversation as they discuss the right word to complete the line: "All he can do is ... and hide."

Sita: I think it's *run*.
Mark: Frogs don't *run*, they *jump*!
Sita: OK - what about *hop* then?
Mark: It's the same isn't it?
Sita: Well, yes - but it sort of matches ... "*hop* and *hide*" ... they begin with the same letter ... the same sound.

The sensitivity to words which Sita and Mark are learning from this activity will enhance all their writing from stories to reports, and will add to their appreciation of stories and poems they read. It will even help them towards Attainment Targets for "Knowledge About Language", for example, Level 5 in the Reading Profile Component:

> *"Recognise and talk about ... some of the effects of the writer's choice of words in imaginative uses of English."*

Sita has recognised the effects of alliteration, though she does not know the word for it yet. Many other aspects of the Programmes of Study and Attainment Targets for Reading are covered in this activity, as are aspects of the Speaking and Listening Profile Component, since oracy is used here as the learning method. Later, when Sita and Mark go on to write their own poems, they will be fulfilling many aspects of the Writing Profile Component.

This sheet, like most others in this book, encourages an ACTIVE approach to poetry based upon reading, listening, speaking and writing - an approach which is endorsed by the Cox Report:

> *"Building on their experiences of reading and hearing a wide range of poetry, they should have opportunities, both individually and in groups, to use poetic features such as rhythm, rhyme and alliteration in verse such as jingles, limericks, ballads, haiku, etc. "*

The important point about poetry teaching, and indeed all aspects of National Curriculum English, is to begin with exciting and worthwhile schemes of work which integrate the language modes, and then relate them to National Curriculum Programmes of Study and Attainment Targets. To work the other way round, i.e. aiming directly at the Attainment Targets, will stultify teaching and be particularly detrimental to poetry.

Finally, if the sheer extent of National Curriculum English seems to be squeezing poetry out, we need only to remind ourselves of the Cox Report:

> *"Poetry needs to be at the heart of work in English because of the quality of language at work on experience that it offers us."*

Twenty Ways to Teach Poetry

1. ACTION POETRY

Getting pupils to act out a poem is a physical response which gives them the opportunity to respond to rhythm and sound, as well as subject matter. It is particularly effective with very young children.

Engines

The train comes rattling round the track
With a clackety-clack
And a rat-a-tat-tat
Pulled by an engine with a big smoke stack
With a clackety-clack
And a rat-a-tat-tat

His connecting rods go round and round
With a clackety-clack
And a rat-a-tat-tat
As he puffs along with a thundering sound
With a clackety-clack
And a rat-a-tat-tat

He's taking his passengers to work and play
With a clackety-clack
And a rat-a-tat-tat
And some lucky people on holiday
With a clackety-clack
And a rat-a-tat-tat.

2. REPETITIVE PATTERNS

Repeated patterns can support memorisation and improvisation. Here is an example:

The Goblin

A goblin lives in our house, in our house, in our house,
A goblin lives in our house all year round.
He bumps
And he jumps
And he thumps
And he stumps
He knocks
And he rocks
And he rattles at the locks.
A goblin lives in our house, in our house, in our house,
A goblin lives in our house all the year round.

Rose Fyleman

Read the poem to the pupils. Help them memorise the first two lines and make up more things that the goblin does. Work in groups to build up the poem from memory/improvisation. Groups can recite their versions to each other. You could extend the poem by using other ideas : "A spider lives in our house..." etc.

3. TONGUE TWISTERS

Use "Peter Piper" or other poems to spark off interest in tongue twisters and ask children to make up their own.

Betty bought a bit of butter.
Betty said,"My butter's bitter.
If I put it in my batter,
It will make my batter bitter.
Better buy some better butter."
Betty's mother said she'd let her.
So she bought some better butter
And it made her batter better.

4. CLAP AND CHOOSE RHYMES

Pupils can share any clapping and choose rhymes they know:

Micky Mouse bought a house,
What colour did he paint it?
Shut your eyes and think.
RED
R-E-D spells red,
And out you must go for saying so
With a clip across your ear-hole.

5. CHORAL POETRY

A group of children can share the reading of a poem using different combinations of voices. It is important to choose poems which lend themselves to this kind of presentation, e.g. Auden's "Night Mail".

6. RHYME TENNIS

Pupils play in pairs facing each other. One pupil "serves" by saying a word and then the other "hits back" by saying a rhyming word. The point is won when one of the children cannot think of a rhyme. It is a good idea to limit the game to a list of words which have a good range of rhymes. Use the same idea to explore alliteration. This is more flexible and there is no need to limit the words.

7. FREE ASSOCIATION TENNIS

This is similar to "Rhyme Tennis", but pupils respond by saying the first word that comes into their heads. This is a good way of exploring connotative meaning and imagery. Ask pupils to jot down any interesting groups of words that came up during the game, so that they can be explored further and perhaps be worked up into a poem.

8. CLERIHEWS

These funny four line poems were invented by Edmund Clerihew Bentley. The first line is a name, and the rest of the poem is developed out of a rhyme with the name. Lines can be of any length.

Daniel Defoe
Lived a long time ago
He had nothing to do, so
He wrote Robinson Crusoe.

9. POETRY AROUND US

Get children to look out for slogans, advertisements, headlines, etc. which use language in an interesting way - rhymes, alliteration, puns, repetition - and use cuttings to make a wall display.

10. KNOCK KNOCK JOKES

Children love these and no doubt will have many examples. They are good for getting across two important points about poetry in an enjoyable way: (a) puns, wordplay: (b) pattern in poetry.

Knock, knock.
Who's there?
Freeze.
Freeze who?
Freeze a jolly good fellow!

11. LIMERICKS

These are great fun and get across a strong sense of rhythm and pattern. They also provide a good way of exploring wordplay and "unconventional" spelling.

There was an old man of Nantucket
Who kept all his cash in a bucket;
But his daughter, named Nan,
Ran away with a man,
And as for the bucket, Nantucket.

12. CONVERSATION POEMS

These are poems based on snatches of conversation:

Says she to me, "Was that you?"
Says I, "Who?"
Says she, "You."
Says I, "Where?"
Says she, "There."
Says I, "When?"
Says she, "Then."
Says I, "No."
Says she, "Oh ..."

Such poems could be built up from "backchat" - pupil talking to teacher, child to parent, or could be a collection of "Things Adults Say" or "Mum's Moans". These poems could also offer an opportunity to practice punctuating direct speech, the repeated pattern forming a supportive framework.

13. A "ZOOM LENS" POEM

This is a descriptive poem of several verses, each verse being a description of what can be seen through the various positions of a zoom lens. Verse 1 begins with a "wide" position, giving a general description of the scene, and each verse moves in closer and closer until the final "tele" position in which part of the scene is described in great detail.

14. OBJECTS WITH FEELINGS

Imagine that the objects around us could think and feel.

The Old Field

The old field is sad
Now the children have gone home.
They have played with him all afternoon,
Kicking the ball to him, and him
Kicking it back.

But now it is growing cold and dark.
He thinks of their warm breath, and their
Feet like little hot-water bottles.
A bit rough, some of them, but still ...

And now, he thinks, there's not even a dog
To tickle me.
The gates are locked.
The birds don't like this nasty sneaking wind,
And nor does he.

D J Enright

15. GENRE SWITCHING

Retell a poem using a different genre, e.g. as a story, as a newspaper article, as a report. Follow this by doing the reverse - turn a description from a history reader into a poem, for example.

16. "COLD POEMS"

Use the following poem and ask the children to "translate" it. They will soon guess that it is what someone with a cold sounds like. Discuss the sounds that are affected by a cold, and why - experiments with nose-pinching will help! - and then get the children to write their own "cold poems".

Lides to Bary Jade (Mary Jane)

The bood is beagig brighdly love,
The sdars are shidig too;
While I ab gazig dreabily
Add thigkig, love, of you;
You caddot, oh, you caddot, kdow,
By darlig, how I biss you -
(Oh, whadt a fearful cold I've got -
Ck-tish-u! Ck-ck-tish-u!)

17. GRAFFITI POEMS

A group of children could pool the graffiti they have seen and perhaps spend some time researching it (you will need to place a ban on the ruder kind!). Finally the group edits its graffiti into an interesting sequence. Final presentations could be done using a variety of handwriting and media - chalk, felt-tipped marker, even spray paint - on a "brick-wall" background.

I like grils.
You mean you like girls.
What's wrong with grils?
Preserve wildlife -
Pickle a squirrel.
Tolkein is hobbit forming.
My mother made me a vandal.
If I bought her the wool
Would she make me one?

18. BALLAD

These can be read or distributed to the class and form the basis for discussion. The ballad is then cut up into individual verses. Give each verse to a pair to produce an illustrated large-text version for display. Reassemble the verses to create a wall display.

19. POETRY ADVERTISEMENTS

Children can browse through class poetry anthologies and choose a poem to advertise. The advertisement should state clearly where the poem can be found, and should use words and pictures to encourage people to read that poem. Advertisements can then be displayed so that children can make their own choices.

20. POETRY TOP TEN

A good follow-up to advertising poems would be to compile a top-ten list of all the poems advertised, and perhaps make poetry "videos" of them.

Nursery Rhymes

Three nursery rhymes have got muddled up. Can you sort them out again? You will need to read each line very carefully.

Hey, diddle, diddle!

Mary, Mary, quite contrary,

How does your garden grow?

The clock struck one,

Hickory, Dickory, Dock,

The cow jumped over the moon.

With silver bells and cockleshells,

To see such sport,

The mouse ran up the clock;

The little dog laughed,

The mouse ran down,

The cat and the fiddle,

And the dish ran away with the spoon.

And pretty maids all in a row.

Hickory, Dickory, Dock.

- Take 2 or 3 more nursery rhymes. Cut the lines into strips, jumble them up and stick them down in the wrong order! Pass them to your partner to sort out!

- Can you make up your own nursery rhymes? Here are some ideas to start you off:

Diddledy, diddledy doo
A frog lived in a shoe ...

Little Mary Anne
Lived in a caravan ...

One misty, moisty morning,
When cloudy was the weather,
There I met an old man
Clothed all in leather;

Clothed all in leather,
With cap under his chin,
How do you do, and how do you do,
And how do you do again!

Sneeze on a Monday, sneeze for danger;
Sneeze on a Tuesday, kiss a stranger;
Sneeze on a Wednesday, get a letter;
Sneeze on a Thursday, something better;
Sneeze on a Friday, sneeze for sorrow;
Sneeze on a Saturday, see your sweetheart tomorrow.

One, two,
Buckle my shoe;
Three, four,
Knock at the door;
Five, six,
Pick up sticks;
Seven, eight,
Lay them straight,
Nine, ten,
A good fat hen.
Eleven, twelve,
Dig and delve;
Thirteen, fourteen,
Maids a-courting;
Fifteen, sixteen,
Maids in the kitchen;
Seventeen, eighteen,
Maids a-waiting;
Nineteen, twenty,
A plate's empty.

There was an old woman toss'd up in a blanket
Nineteen times as high as the moon;
Where she was going I couldn't but ask it,
For in her hand she carried a broom.

"Old woman, old woman, old woman," quoth I,
"O wither, O wither, O wither, so high?"
"To sweep the cobwebs off the sky!"
"Shall I go with thee?" "Ay, by-and-by."

Thirty days hath September,
April, June and November;
February has twenty-eight alone,
All the rest have thirty-one,
Excepting leap-year, that's the time
When February's days are twenty-nine.

Peter Piper picked a peck of pickled pepper;
A peck of pickled pepper Peter Piper picked;
If Peter Piper picked a peck of pickled pepper;
Where's the peck of pickled pepper Peter Piper picked?

As I was going to St. Ives,
I met a man with seven wives;
Each wife had seven sacks,
Each sack had seven cats,
Each cat had seven kits:
Kits, cats, sacks, and wives,
How many were going to St. Ives?

BEST ✂ WORDS

Choose the best words to fill the spaces. Cut out the words you have chosen and stick them in place.

"I can't bite
like a dog,"
said the bright
green_____

spider | dog
elephant | frog

"I can't nip,
I can't_____
I can't grip
I can't hurt.

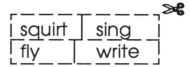

squirt | sing
fly | write

"All I can do,
is _____and hide
when enemies come
from far and wide.

run | jump
hop | wriggle

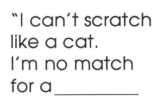

"I can't scratch
like a cat.
I'm no match
for a_____

frog | rat
hat | rhinoceros

"I can't stab
I can't snare,
I can't grab
I can't _____

frighten | scare
hurt | fight

"All I can do
my whole life through
is hop," said the_____ ,
"and hide from view."

And that's
what I saw him
up and do.

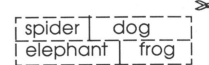

spider | dog
elephant | frog

● Read ALOUD your poem to a partner. Does it SOUND right?
Do you want to make any changes?

● Make up a poem using some of your left-over words.

Arrange the animals in alphabetical order down the page. When you have done this, write something to describe each animal.

ANTELOPES leap gracefully
BABOONS chatter like hairy old men
COBRAS coil and slither

_____
_____
_____
_____
_____
_____
_____
_____
_____
_____
_____
_____
_____
_____
_____
_____
_____
_____
_____
_____
_____
_____
_____
_____
_____
_____

HIPPOS
QUAILS
RATTLESNAKES
SEALS
WHALES
FISH
JAGUARS
OCTOPI
ELEPHANTS
INSECTS
PARROTS
TARANTULAS
UNICORNS
KOALA BEARS
GORILLAS
DOGS
LIONS
NEWTS
MONKEYS
YAKS
VOLES
ZEBRAS

●Which letter is missing from your poem? Can you find an animal whose name starts with that letter?

●Read your poem ALOUD to a partner. Does it SOUND right? Do you want to make any changes?

●Write some more alphabet poems. Here are some ideas:

FOOD HORRORS	NAMES	THINGS I LIKE CHRISTMAS PRESENTS

Simple Poetry Snap.

ate	eight	great	wait
chalk	stalk	squawk	hawk
cap	lap	yap	zap
day	grey	stay	say
bee	key	sea	chimpanzee
scream	moonbeam	gleam	steam

This page may be photocopied for classroom use only

Simple Poetry Snap.

jam	lamb	swam	pram
star	car	guitar	far
catch	match	scratch	patch
crane	rain	brain	drain
hair	nightmare	square	there
ache	bake	cake	make

THE ALLIRAFFEBUTTEROG

Chloe and Zoe wrote this poem about a very strange creature ...

The Alliraffebutterog has the neck of a giraffe,
And the head of a dog.
Butterfly wings, alligator's tail,
Nobody knows whether it's male or female.

People come for miles to see
This marvellous friend that belongs mostly to me.
People take pictures - the news and the press,
The Alliraffebutterog is surely the best!
But soon it goes back to its family
Down in the depths of Butterogany.

Chloe and Zoe

First, they chose four creatures:

an alligator, a giraffe, a butterfly and a dog.

The next stage was to take one part from each name:

<u>ALLI</u>GATOR
GI<u>RAFFE</u>
<u>BUTTER</u>FLY
D<u>OG</u>

They created an Alliraffebutterog!

Then they chose the parts of the creature's bodies which went together and drew a picture.

Finally they wrote a poem about it.

 ●You try it!

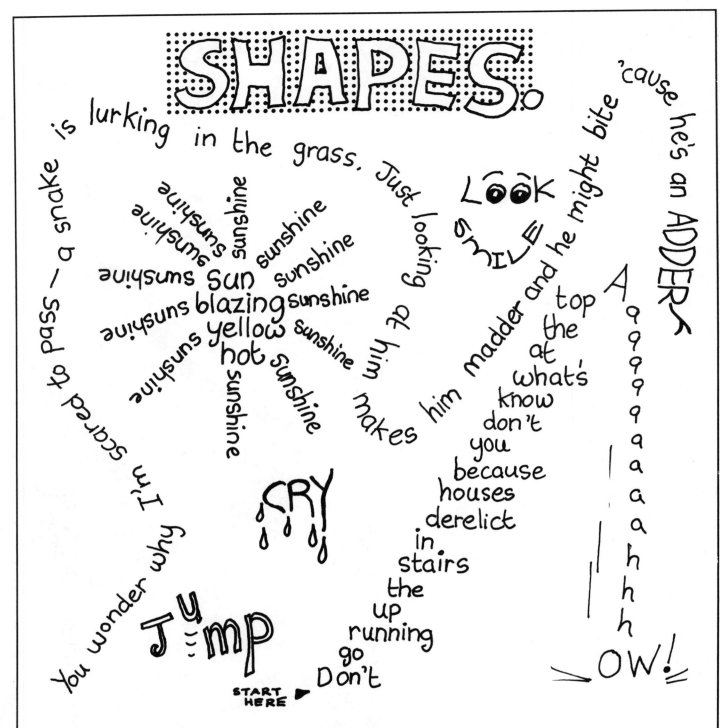

SHAPES

a snake is lurking in the grass. Just looking at him makes him madder and he might bite 'cause he's an ADDER

You wonder why I'm scared to pass — a snake

LOOK SMILE

sunshine sunshine sunshine sunshine sunshine sunshine sunshine Sun sunshine blazing sunshine sunshine yellow sunshine hot sunshine sunshine sunshine

A a a a a a a a h h h OW!

top
the
at
what's
know
don't
you
because
houses
derelict
in
stairs
the
up
running
go
Don't

CRY

JUmp

START HERE ▶

Look at the shape of these poems. What do you notice?

NOW ●Try writing your own shape poems. Here are some ideas:

WATERFALL	TRAIN	EYE	TREE
STAR	SKELETON	FACE	HAND

●Notice how the words LOOK, SMILE, CRY and JUMP have been brought to life.

●Try this with other words and use them in your shape poems or other writing.

POETRY FORMATS 1

A Radio Alarm Poem

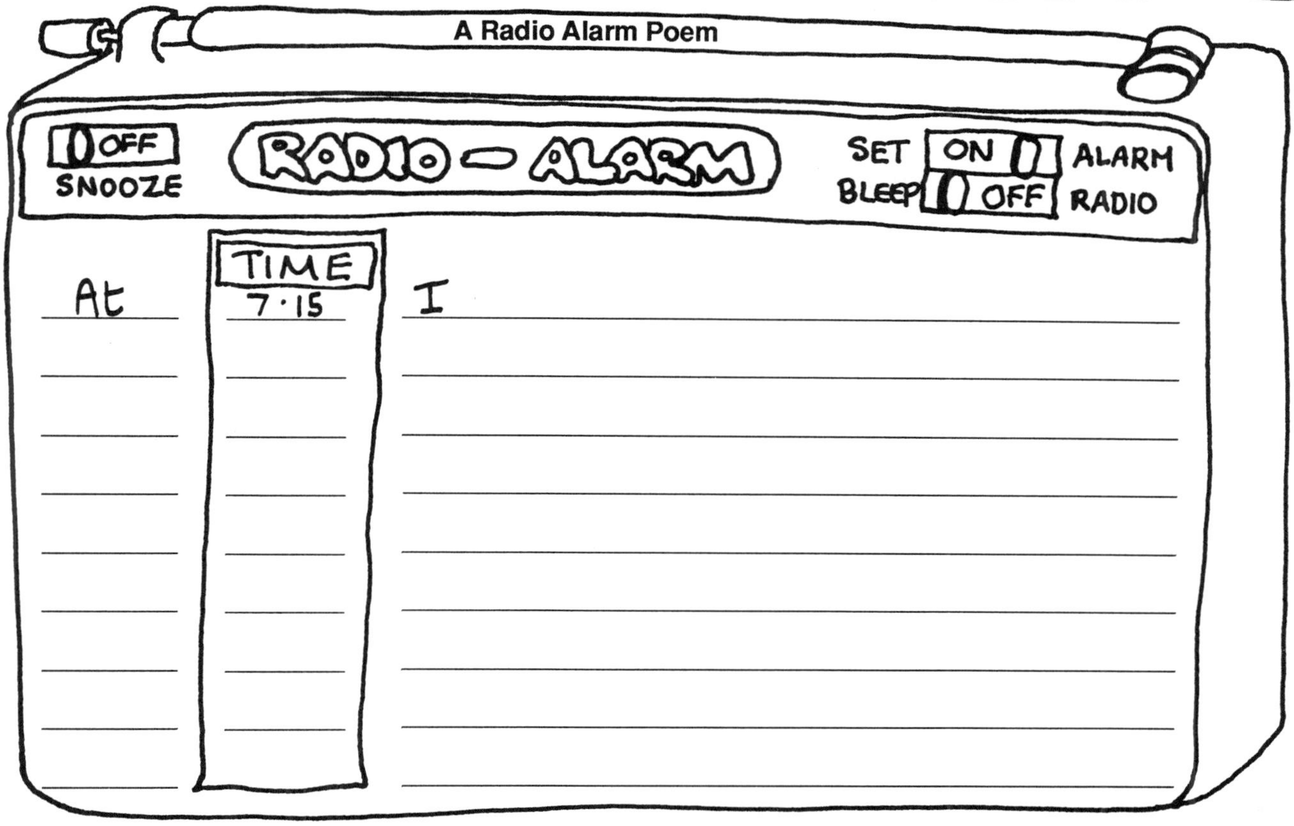

OFF
SNOOZE

RADIO – ALARM

SET   ON   ALARM
BLEEP OFF   RADIO

At _____   **TIME** 7·15   I _____

A Diary Poem

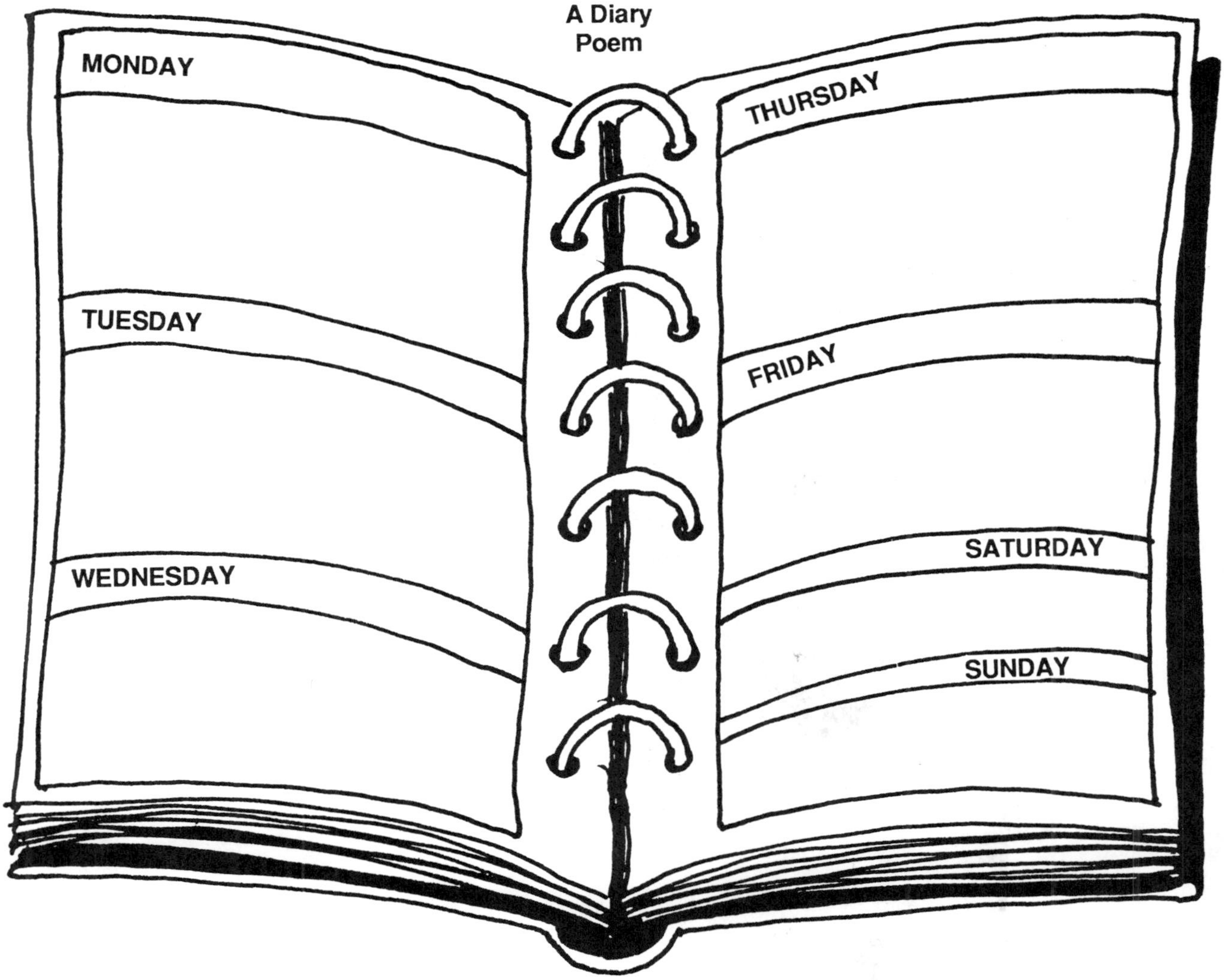

MONDAY

TUESDAY

WEDNESDAY

THURSDAY

FRIDAY

SATURDAY

SUNDAY

POETRY FORMATS 2

Get into pairs and write your names in the "names" boxes. Agree on a subject and write it in the "subject" box. Write as many words for that subject as you can think of in the columns A and B. Compare notes and get more ideas, then fill in columns C and D. Use the longer boxes to jot down words and phrases, and the scratchpad for notes. Finally write your poem on the computer screen You could have a class exhibition of all the poems produced in this way.

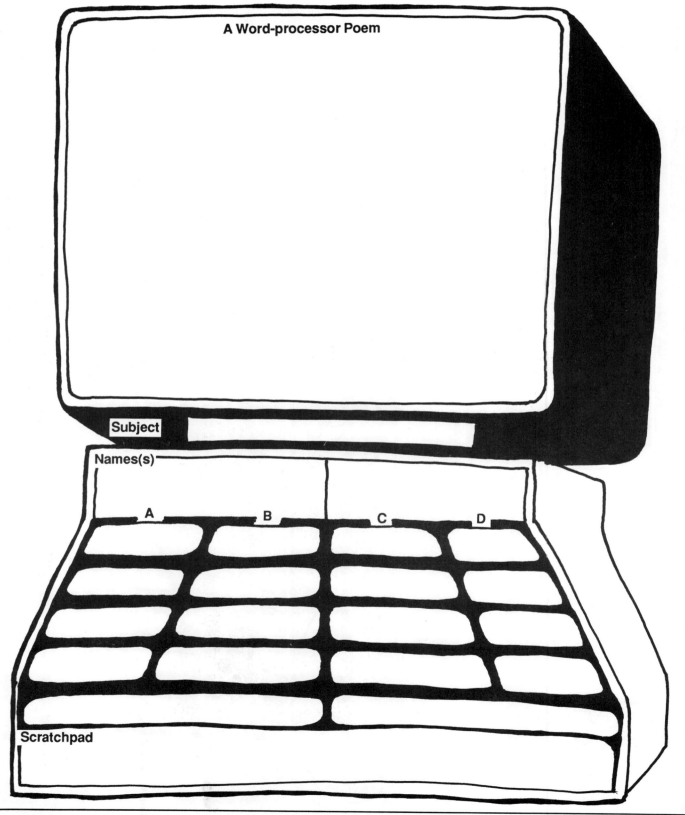

A Word-processor Poem

Subject

Names(s)

A   B   C   D

Scratchpad

NEWSPAPER POEMS

Rolling thunder

A SHOWER

LONG

LONGER

Wet, wet, wet

Electryifying efforts!

WHAT A STORMER

Swan Lake

WET WET WET

TOP THAT

NOW ● Choose one idea from the IDEAS BOX.

FOOD	CARS MUSIC	DISASTERS SPORT

● Collect some newspapers and cut out any headlines which match your idea.

● Put them in order to make your own poem.

GHOSTBUSTERS

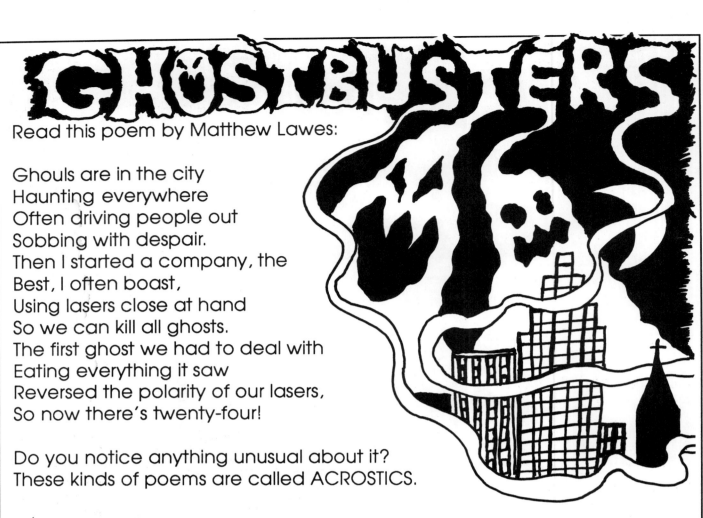

Read this poem by Matthew Lawes:

Ghouls are in the city
Haunting everywhere
Often driving people out
Sobbing with despair.
Then I started a company, the
Best, I often boast,
Using lasers close at hand
So we can kill all ghosts.
The first ghost we had to deal with
Eating everything it saw
Reversed the polarity of our lasers,
So now there's twenty-four!

Do you notice anything unusual about it?
These kinds of poems are called ACROSTICS.

● Write an acrostic of your own. Here are some ideas for you to choose from:

SUN	RAIN	SCHOOL
NIGHT	CAT	

● Even harder - write one using your own name and telling somebody about YOU!
You could colour in or decorate the first letter of every line.
Plan a display of all the poems for your classroom.

● With a partner find the missing first letters in the two poems here. What words do they spell?

oon climbs up
ver the top of a hill, and sits
n the top of a chimney pot
ear my house.

The word is: _____

pooks and ghouls
arade the night
n the staircases
h what a fright! So when alone
eep the doors locked at night!

The word is: _____

MAGIC SPELLS

This is the magic spell chanted by the three evil witches in Shakespeare's play, "*Macbeth*". But all the ingredients have been left out!
Make the spell work by writing in your own ingredients.

Round about the cauldron go;
In the_____throw:
_____ that under cold stone
Days and nights has thirty-one.

_____
Boil thou first in the charmed pot!

Double, double toil and trouble;
Fire burn and cauldron bubble.
Fillet of a_____
In the cauldron boil and bake,
Eye of_____ and toe of _____
Wool of_____and tongue of _____
_____ sting
_____ wing
For a charm of powerful trouble
Like a hell-broth, boil and bubble.

Double, double, toil and trouble;
Fire burn and cauldron bubble.

_____
_____
_____
_____
Cool it with a baboon's blood
Then the charm is firm and good!

Written by William Shakespeare and

_____
(write your name here.)

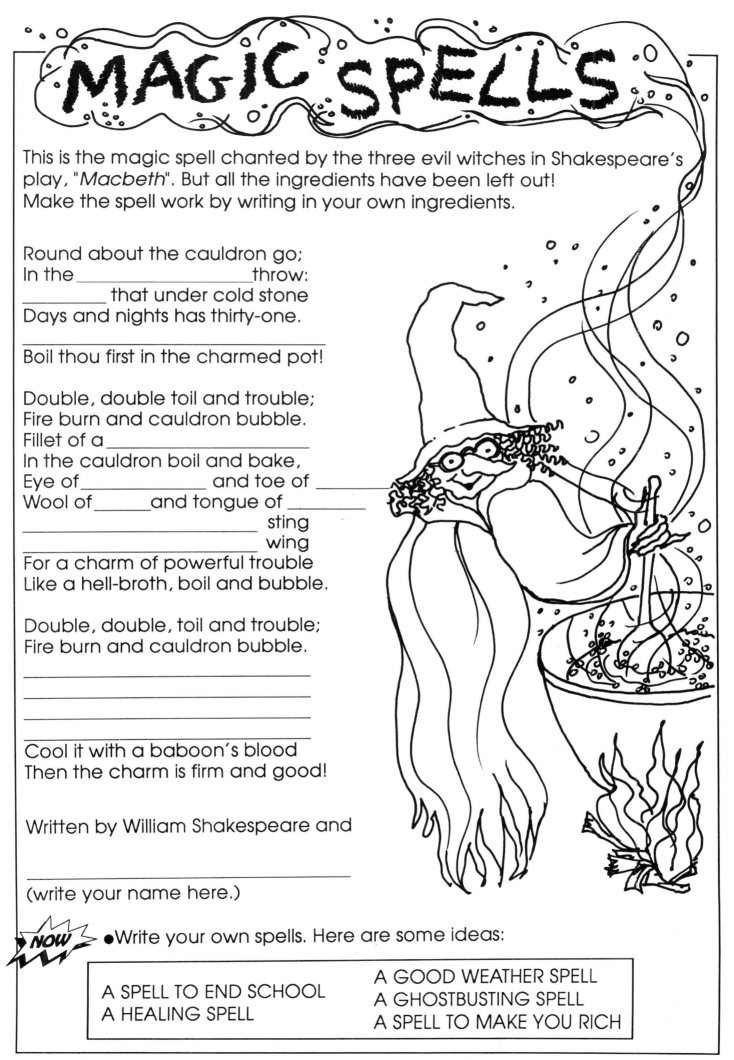

NOW ●Write your own spells. Here are some ideas:

A SPELL TO END SCHOOL
A HEALING SPELL

A GOOD WEATHER SPELL
A GHOSTBUSTING SPELL
A SPELL TO MAKE YOU RICH

This page may be photocopied for classroom use only

HAIKU

Long before cars and videos were imported from Japan, English poets borrowed a kind of poetry called HAIKU.

Here is an example:

> Haiku are icebergs:
> Three lines floating on the page,
> The rest unwritten.

Since haiku are so short, not a word can be wasted, and the words that are written need to hint at much more.

The haiku is based on SYLLABLES. A syllable is a part of a word with its own sound. "Page" has one syllable, "iceberg" has two syllables.

- Say your name ALOUD to a partner.
- Ask him or her to count the number of syllables in your name.

Here is the challenge! A haiku MUST have seventeen syllables in this order:

> Evenings ornament 5
> The golden medallion 7
> Of the setting sun. 5

Here are four horrific haiku which have been jumbled up. Use your knowledge to sort them out.

> The full moon shines bright
> To haunt the night sky
> Is that shape in the shadows
> A mosquito bite.
> A trick of the light?
> A zig-zag on vampire wings
> A murmur, a sigh, a knock
> Footsteps on the stair
> Of blood - was my nightmare true
> But no-one is there
> A vampire drained me
> Bird? No bird would fly

- Write some haiku of your own.
  When you have finished, you might like to present them for display using any Japanese writing or pictures you can find.

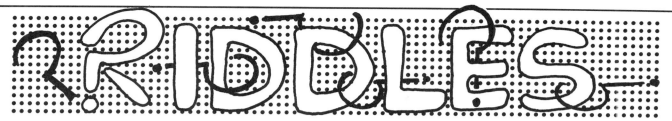

RIDDLES

QUESTION: How did people spend their evenings before television was invented?
ANSWER: They made their own entertainment!

One way they did this was to tell riddles to each other. Here is a riddle over a thousand years old!

> I saw a creature who feeds cattle,
> It has many teeth,
> It goes pointing downwards,
> It searches the soil, seeking herbs,
> Always finding those which are not firm
> But leaving the fair ones fixed,
> Gleaming brightly, blowing and growing.

Can you guess the answer?
The answer is:_____

Sometimes a clue was given in the form of a word-puzzle. Read this riddle carefully:

> WOB is my name, if you work it out;
> I'm a fair creature fashioned for battle.
> When I bend, and shoot a deadly shaft
> From my stomach, I desire only to send
> That poison as far away as possible.
> No man is parted easily from the object
> I describe; if he's struck by what flies
> From my stomach, he pays for its poison
> With his strength - or even with his life.

Can you guess the answer?
The answer is: _____

Another ancient way of giving a clue was to give the answer in the runic alphabet.

| ᚠ ᚢ ᚦ ᛖ ᚱ ᛚ ᚷ ᛈ ᚺ ᛏ ᛁ ᚲ ᛉ ᛏ ᛒ ᛗ ᚫ ᛚ ᛞ ᚲ ᛘ |
| F U th O R ᴅκ G W H N I/J P S T B E M L D A Y |

- Write some Anglo-Saxon type riddles of your own or pass secret messages to each other using runes.

- Write out your best riddles and messages for display.

WAYS OF LOOKING

Poetry often helps us look at ordinary things in new ways.

The television aerials
In our street
Look like
A row of
Chinese writing.

Granddad's
Shiny bald head
Looks like
The egg
I had for my breakfast.

Complete these two unfinished "Looks like ..." poems:

The tree branches
Bare of leaves
Look like

The snow that
Covers our garden
Looks like

_____

_____

_____

_____

Fun, aren't they? Now make up some of your own. Work in pairs and write beginnings for each other to finish off.

Now you are ready for something more ambitious - doing the same thing six times over in one poem! Here is an example:

SIX WAYS OF LOOKING AT A TENNIS BALL

It is an old man with a bald head
and a smiling face

It is our world, and that black speck
is me

It is a moon fallen from orbit

It is a precious pearl from the
depths of the sea

It is a crystal ball in which
I might see the future

It is the largest gobstopper
in the world - gulp!

NOW ● Write your own SIX WAYS OF LOOKING AT A ... poem. It might be good to work with a partner for your first attempt.

Description

Read these two poems carefully:

It is made of wood
It has a roundish shape
A bit bigger than a dinner plate
With a handle bound with black tape
The round frame
Is threaded
With criss-cross nylon.

A smash hit!
Looking like a flattened guitar
Criss-crossed with spaghetti strings,
It's the latest Wimbledon craze
And everyone in the top ten's got one!

Can you guess what the poet is describing?

I think the poet is describing a _____

The poet started by taking a simple object and describing it in two ways.
Here are his notes:

FACTUAL

1. Made of : wood - strings are nylon usually
2. Shape: round - handle long and thin
3. Size : size of dinner plate
4. Colour: brown - depends - handle bound with black tape.

IMAGINATIVE

1. Strings remind me of spaghetti
2. Shape reminds me of a guitar, but it is much flatter
3. Usually seen at Wimbledon
4. Smashes tennis balls around courts.

A

B

NOW

- Choose ONE of these pictures and make notes to describe it in the two ways shown above.

- Turn your rough notes into a poem with two verses.

- Try the same idea on a number of everyday objects - a book, a chair, a ruler.
  If you leave out the name of the object, it can be a riddle.
  Can your partner guess what the object is?

SOUNDS

This poem is based on the sounds people make.

You have been given the first and the last verses. Cut up the rest and fit the lines together so you have a complete poem.

Jibber, jabber, gabble, babble,
Cackle, clack and prate,
Twiddle, twaddle, mutter, stutter,
Utter, splutter, blate.

Spiel and spout and spit it out

Snicker, snort and snap

Chew the rag and crack

Grumble, mumble moan

Gab and gag and groan

Sniffle, snuffle, drawl and bawl

Chin and chirp and chat

Shout and shoot and gargle, gasp

Chatter, patter, tattle, prattle

Hem and haw and work the jaw

Bark and buzz and yap and yelp

Tell the world and quack

**FIT THE LINES TOGETHER
IN THIS SPACE**

Beef and bellyache and bat,
Say a mouthful, squawk,
That is what some people do
When they merely talk.

Make up a title for this poem. My title is: _____

NOW ●Think of other sounds that people make and write one or two
extra verses for the poem.

●Write a similar poem based on animal sounds.

This page may be photocopied for classroom use only

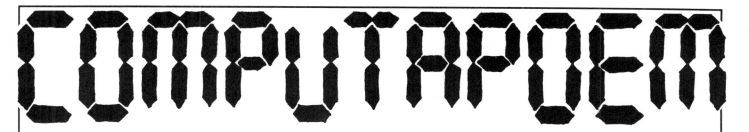

COMPUTAPOEM

INSTRUCTIONS: 1. Cut out the word strips and thread them through the display slots so that the sets of words can be seen. (See the diagram.)

	DISPLAY 1	**ADJECTIVE**	**NOUN**
I LIKE TO	_ _ _ _ _ _ _ _ _ _ _ _ _ _ _ _ _ _	_ _ _ _ _ _ _ _ _ _ _ _ _ _ _ _ _ _	_ _ _ _ _ _ _ _ _ _ _ _ _ _ _ _ _ _

2. Now pull through the strips to select a line of poetry in DISPLAY 1. You will find another line of poetry has appeared in DISPLAY 2 and that this actually rhymes with line 1!

3. These are lines 2 and 4 of a four line poem. Your job is to write lines 1 and 3 in such a way as to bring the whole verse together as best you can. It won't make much sense, but you can create some surprising lines!

Make sure you can pull the strip through.
You should only see your word in the slot.

	DISPLAY 2	**ADJECTIVE**	**NOUN**
I LIKE TO	_ _ _ _ _ _ _ _ _ _ _ _ _ _ _ _ _ _	_ _ _ _ _ _ _ _ _ _ _ _ _ _ _ _ _ _	_ _ _ _ _ _ _ _ _ _ _ _ _ _ _ _ _ _

● Make up your own wordstrips. Write programs for subjects such as SCIENCE FICTION, HORROR, ANIMALS, SCHOOL.

● Design a wordstrip program which makes sensible lines of poetry every time.

CUT INTO STRIPS AND THREAD THROUGH THE COMPUTAPOEM SHEET

eat	hairy	computers
drink	beautiful	food
taste	powerful	pop songs
touch	tasty	creatures
daydream about	green	cakes
talk to	delicious	books
watch films about	tiny	trousers
read about	refreshing	trees
joke about	interesting	lawn mowers
write poems about	the latest	ghouls
kiss	trendy	clothes
wear	fascinating	peaches
go on holiday with	good looking	commuters
make friends with	tired	blood
draw	red	billabongs
take photos of	sticky	features
listen to	ugly	snakes
own	slippery	spooks
sit next to	miserable	houses
pose with	slimy	bees
learn about	complicated	party-goers
buy	dangerous	swimming pools

BALLADS

A ballad is a story told in verse. Long ago, when most people were unable to read and write, stories were passed on in this way because they were easy to remember. "The Outlandish Knight" came down to us in this way.

It is printed here with all the verses jumbled up. Cut out the verses and put them together again in the right order.

Then she mounted on her lilywhite horse
And quickly rode away
And she arrived at her father's house
Before the break of day.

At last they came to the river's side
"This is the place!" cried he,
"For six pretty maids I've drowned here before
And the seventh you shall be.

An outlandish knight came from the north lands
And he came wooing of me.
He said he would take me to foreign lands
Where he would marry me.

"Lie there, lie there, you false-hearted man,
Lie there instead of me
For six pretty maids you have drowned here before
But the seventh has drownded thee!

She mounted on her lilywhite horse
And he upon the grey,
And they did ride to the river side
Three hours ere it was day.

She said, "I beg you to crop the thistle
That grows beside the brim
That it may not tangle my curly locks
Nor scratch my lilywhite skin.

"Now go and get me your father's gold
And some of your mother's fee,
And two of the very best stable steeds
To ride on our long journey."

"Take off, take off your silken gown,
Take off your dainty shoe,
For they're much too rich to rot in a ditch
As you are sure to do.

So she got a sickle to crop the thistle
That grew beside the brim
And as she turned round she pushed him down
And tumbled him into the stream.

NOW

● Prepare the ballad for a group presentation. One person could read the part of the knight, another the girl, and a third, the narrator.

● In Part II of the ballad, (not printed here), the girl tries to keep her strange adventure a secret, but her father notices mud on her gown and sweat on her horse. Write your own version of Part II - it need not be in poetry - and make up your own ending.

"The Outlandish Knight" has recently been retold as a short story. This is how it begins:

Hearing a clatter of hooves in the courtyard, Laura looked out of her window to see what all of the fuss was about. She was surprised to see a strange knight clad in chain mail and a grotesque boar-crested helmet. She was even more surprised when she heard him say in a strange northern accent, "I have come to ask for your daughter's hand in marriage."

She heard her father reply cautiously, "Well sir, we are honoured but perhaps it would be better if we got to know each other first - stay for a few days."

If Laura had been impressed by the sight of this knight in his armour, she was even more impressed when she saw him without his helmet - he was young, handsome, and his conversation was charming. She felt annoyed that her slow, cautious father had not accepted his offer straight away, and feared that he might change his mind and leave.

Laura had a strange dream that night in which her handsome suitor embraced her and then turned into a devil. She woke suddenly to the sound of tapping at her door and a moment later the knight was standing beside her.

"Forgive me," he said, "but I must return to my lands tonight. I would like to take you with me, but your father ..."

"He only wants the best for me," interrupted Laura.

"He has nothing to fear," said the knight. "I am a prince in my own lands and have a castle and great wealth."

Laura's heart pounded. Should she betray her father and accept? And what about her dreams? One look at the knight's handsome face helped her to make up her mind - yes, she would go, and when she returned a princess she would

- ●Prepare this story for a group presentation. One person could read the part of the knight, and others, the girl, her father, and the narrator.

- ●What are the differences between the story and the ballad?
  Look particularly at:
  the shape
  the amount of detail
  the description
  the dialogue
  the style of writing

- ●Continue the modern version of the story in the same style.
  As the final story will be quite long, it will be a good idea to work on it as a group and to divide the story between you.

Resource sheet - Ballads.

The Derby Ram

As I was going to Derby, sir,
Upon a market day,
I saw the biggest ram, sir,
That ever was fed on hay.

And indeed, sir,'tis true, sir,
I never was given to lie
And if you'd been in Derby, sir,
You'd have seen him as well as I.

This ram was fat behind, sir,
This ram was fat before,
He measured ten yards round, sir,
If not a little more.

He had four feet to walk on, sir,
He had four feet to stand,
And every foot he had, sir,
Did cover an acre of land.

The man who killed this ram, sir,
Was drowned all in the blood,
And he who held the dish, sir,
Was carried away in the flood.

The mutton that ram made, sir,
Gave all the army meat,
And what was left, I'm told , sir,
Was served out to the fleet.

The wool grew on his back, sir,
It reached up to the sky,
And there the eagles built their nests,
I heard the young ones cry.

The wool grew on his belly, sir,
It reached down to the ground.
And that was sold in Derby town
For forty thousand pound.

The horns upon this ram, sir,
They reached up to the moon.
A little boy went up in January
And he never got back till June.

And all the boys of Derby
Came begging for his eyes,
To make themselves some footballs
For they were of football size.

Traditional

The Streets of Laredo

As I walked out in the streets of Laredo,
As I walked out in Laredo one day,
I spied a young cowboy all wrapped in white linen,
All wrapped in white linen as cold as clay.

"I see by your outfit that you are a cowboy" -
Those words he did say as I boldly stepped by,
"Come sit down beside me and hear my sad story;
I'm shot in the breast and I know I must die.

It was once in the saddle I used to go dashing,
Once in the saddle I was used to stay,
First to the ale-house and then to the jail-house,
Got shot in the breast and I'm dying today.

Get six jolly cowboys to carry my coffin;
Get six pretty maidens to carry my pall;
Put bunches of roses all over my coffin,
Roses to deaden the clods as they fall.

Oh, beat the drum slowly and play the fife lowly,
Play the dead march as you carry me along;
Take me to the green valley and lay the turf o'er me,
For I'm a young cowboy and I know I've done wrong.

Go gather round you a crowd of young cowboys
And tell them the story of this, my sad fate;
Tell one and the other before they go further
To stop their wild roving before it's too late.

Go fetch me a cup, a cup of cold water
To cool my parched lips," the cowboy then said.
Before I returned, the spirit had left him
And gone to its maker - the cowboy was dead.

We beat the drum slowly and played the fife lowly,
And bitterly wept as we carried him along;
For we all loved our comrade, so brave, young and handsome,
We all loved our comrade although he'd done wrong.

American traditional

ACCENT AND DIALECT

DIALECT = differences in the words used and in grammar.
ACCENT = differences in the way you pronounce words.

Read this poem ALOUD to a partner.

T' WHITE MICE

Ah've upset me Mother - she isn't 'arf mad,
She's walloped me backside, an' telled me eh'm bad.
Ah'm upstairs i' bed wi' noa tea, an' noa spice,
An' all 'cos eh showed owd Miss Jenkins me mice.

Miss Jenkins 'ahr teeacher, she called in terday
Ter talk ter me Mother abaht t' Chapel Play.
Ah went fer me white mice - Rebecca an' Fred,
An' dash it, it's their fault ah'm up 'ere 'i bed.

Ah just popped 'em down on Miss Jenkinses lap,
It worrn't my fault the' fell aht o'me cap;
She should 'a kept still then there'd be nowt ter tell,
But she jumped up an' gave one big almighty yell.

She wor up on that table like t'crack of a gun,
Though ah tried ter tell 'er mice luvss bits o'fun,
But she danced an' she screamed, an' then lost 'er 'at,
It fell inter t'chip pan amoung t'boiling fat.

Miss Jenkins looked funny - all white rahnd 'er lips
While 'er 'at went on cooking among t'blooming chips.
Me Mother sat dahn, she went week in her legs
An' 'er eyes - the' stick oht just like chapel 'at pegs.

Ah've told owd Miss Jenkins ah'm sorry an' that
Ah'll giver me savins ter buy a new 'at.
Wish me Mother worn't mad though - it i'nt sernice,
All ah did wor ter show ahr schooil teacher me mice.

B. Shackleton

You probably found it quite difficult. Why?

Do you recognise the dialect which this poem is written in?

- Pick out the words which are different from those you would use.
  Do you say "spice"? If not, what is your word for "sweets"?

- Sometimes the words are the same as in ordinary English - we call this
  STANDARD ENGLISH - but they have been spelled differently to show
  you how to pronounce them. Pick out some of these words.

ACCENT AND DIALECT

DIALECT = differences in the words used and in grammar.
ACCENT = differences in the way you pronounce words.

Read the poems on this page and decide whether they are examples of dialects or accents.

1. From New York.

The bird song

>   Toity poiple boids
>   Sitt'n on der coib,
>   A' choipin and a'boipin
>   An' eat'n doity woims.

Spring in New York

>   Der spring is sprung,
>   Der grass is riz.
>   I wonder where dem boidies is?
>
>   Der liddle boids is on der wing.
>   Ain't dat absoid?
>   Der liddle wings is on der boid.

2. From London.

>   Wot a marf 'e'd got.
>   Wot a marf.
>   When 'e was a kid,
>   Goo' Lor' luv'll
>   'Is pore old muvver
>   Must 'a' fed 'im wiv a shuvvle.
>
>   Wot a gap 'e'd got.
>   Pore chap,
>   'E'd never been known to larf,
>   'Cos if 'e did
>   It's a penny to a quid
>   'E'd 'a' split 'is fice in 'arf.

3. From the Caribbean.

Linstead Market

>   Carry me ackee a Linstead market;
>   Not a quatty wut sell.
>   Carry me ackee go a Linstead market;
>   Not a quatty wut sell.
>   Lard, wat a night, not a bite,
>   Wat a Satiday night.
>   Lard, wat a night, noy a bite,
>   Wat a Satiday night.
>
>   Everybody come feel up, feel up;
>   Not a quatty wut well.
>   Everybody come feel up, squeeze up;
>   Not a quatty wut sell.
>   Lard, wat a night, not a bite,
>   Wat a Satiday night.
>   Lard, wat a night, not a bite,
>   Wat a Satiday night.

NOW

● Try rewriting these poems in Standard English. What differences do you notice?

● Listen to yourself or a partner reading any of these poems out loud. Try using a tape-recorder.

Christine wrote this piece about her room.

MY ROOM

The best thing about my room is the view. From my window I can see the sea, white seagulls wheeling and sometimes distant ships. And when I'm feeling fed-up I imagine I'm out there sailing away from all my problems.

Here is the same piece set out as poetry. If you work in pairs, your partner could read this out.

MY ROOM

The best thing about my room
Is the view.
From my window I can see
The sea
And sometimes
Distant ships
And when I'm feeling fed-up
I imagine I'm out there
Sailing away from my problems.

- Can you hear any differences between the two readings?
- Read the two pieces again and REALLY listen this time!

POETRY DOES NOT HAVE TO RHYME!

Free verse is only poetry that is free from such problems such as rhyme. The only special feature is that it is set out in lines. Poets use the setting out in lines to make you see and read the words in a different, more thoughtful way.

This page may be photocopied for classroom use only

Free Verse 2

 ● Work with your partner to decide how to set out the following passage as free verse.

HINTS:

✔ Lines should not be longer than can be said in one breath.
✔ Use the lines to create pauses you wish your reader to make.
✔ Emphasise any patterns - for example you can repeat words.
✔ Keep reading it out to hear if it SOUNDS right.
✔ Do not be afraid to keep changing what you have written.

Posters on the wall, Bros, Jason, Kylie, Madonna. My mum doesn't like them, but what does she expect – a framed portrait of the Queen! My desk in the corner cluttered up with pens and pencils, cassettes and Coke cans, school books and smelly socks. My mum says, "How can you work in that mess?" The truth is I don't intend to - I do enough at school! There are things all over the floor, clothes, cake crumbs, another Coke can, my cassette recorder. My Mum says it will get trodden on if I don't pick it up - it doesn't work anyway! That's my room. My Mum says it looks like an earthquake's hit it, but she's wrong – no earthquake could make this much mess!

When you have finished, compare your version with another pair, or with the poet's own version.

● You are ready to write your own free verse poem on the same subject.

- ✂ - - -

MY ROOM

Posters on the wall,
Bros, Jason,
Kylie, Madonna,
My mum doesn't like them,
But what does she expect -
A framed portrait of the Queen!

My desk in the corner
Cluttered up with
Pens and pencils,
Cassettes and Coke cans,
School books and smelly socks.
My mum says, "How can you
work in that mess?"
The truth is I don't intend to
(I do enough at school!)

There are things all over the floor
Clothes
Cake crumbs
Another Coke can
My cassette recorder.
My mum says it'll get trodden on
if I don't pick it up
(It doesn't work anyway!)

That's my room.
My mum says it looks like an
earthquake's hit it
But she's wrong -
No earthquake could make this
much mess!

This page may be photocopied for classroom use only

L I S T POEMS

List poems are probably the easiest poems to write.

Disappointment is waking up and realising it's Monday.
Disappointment is rain at playtime - again.
Disappointment is going on a school trip and having to write about it.
Disappointment is PE when it's freezing.
Disappointment is having to redraft your story when you thought it was finished.
Disappointment is school dinners.
Disappointment is when the football is replaced by a Party Political Broadcast.
Disappointment is missing the late night horror film because it's school tomorrow.
Disappointment is when you get home next day and find you have recorded the wrong channel.
Disappointment is a way of life!

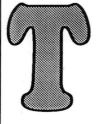

Here's how to write one in a group.

✔ Talk only - no writing allowed!
✔ Agree on your idea.

BOREDOM IS ...	SURPRISE IS ...
HAPPINESS IS ...	A GOOD TIME IS ...
HUMOUR IS ...	ANGER IS ...
	RED IS ...

✔ Each member of the group makes up a line.
✔ Take it in turns to say your line ALOUD.
✔ Add even more lines in your group.
✔ Talk about your lines. Do they sound right?
    Do you want to make any changes?

● Perform your finished poem to the class.

● Write out your poem for display.

Blanks for list poems.

_____ is _____

_____ is _____

_____ is _____

_____ is _____

_____ is _____

_____ is _____

_____ is _____

_____ is _____

_____ is _____

_____ is _____

- ✂

_____ is _____

_____ is _____

_____ is _____

_____ is _____

_____ is _____

_____ is _____

_____ is _____

_____ is _____

_____ is _____

_____ is _____

The worst poet in the world

One of the poems on this page was written by William Worthless of Orpington, who some say is the worst poet in the world.

Read the four poems carefully to decide which poem it is.
What is bad about it?
Why are the other poems so much better?

The Wild Hog

There is a wild hog in the wood,
He kills the men and drinks their blood.

There he comes through yonder marsh,
He splits his way through oak and ash.

Bangum drew his wooden knife,
To rob that wild hog of his life.

They fought four hours of the day,
At length that wild hog stole away.

They followed that wild hog to his den,
And there they found the bones of a
thousand men.

Windy Nights

Whenever the moon and stars are set,
Whenever the wind is high,
All night long in the dark and wet,
A man goes riding by.
Late in the night when the fires are out,
Why does he gallop and gallop about?

Whenever the trees are crying aloud.
And ships are tossed at sea,
By, on the highway, low and loud,
By at the gallop goes he.
By at the gallop he goes and then
By he comes back at the gallop again.

The Frog and the Princess

Once there was a little frog
Who wished that he could be a dog
("A Prince" is what I meant to say
But "dog" was put to rhyme with "frog").

To be a prince the little frog
Had to kiss a pretty hog,
(A "princess" is what I'm trying to say
But "princess" will not rhyme with
"frog" either).

But when he did, the little frog
Got clobbered with a heavy log
And changed into - no, not a Prince -
But just a pile of frog-meat mince.

The Eagle

He clasps the crag with crooked hands;
Close to the sun in lonely lands,
Ringed with the azure world he stands.

The wrinkled sea beneath him crawls;
He watches from his mountain walls,
And like a thunderbolt he falls.

Which poem did you like best? What did you like about it?

● Make a list of four or five things which make a good poem.
  Compare your ideas with another group's.

● Organise a class poetry competition.

Difficult Poetry Snap

SAY	TEA-TRAY	CASTAWAY
whisper shout exclaim reply laugh mutter mumble recite	Twinkle, twinkle little bat, How I wonder what you're at, Up above the sky so high Like a tea-tray in the sky. *Lewis Carroll*	

TAKE-AWAY	CHEVROLET	HOLIDAY
Oh mum! Let's not have chips today, I'd rather have a take-away Flavoured with oriental spice Or with some other stuff's that's nice. Indian, Chinese or Super-Mac I don't really care what they've got As long as it's piping hot. So don't take ages walking back! Just think mum, within our street There's stuff from all the world to eat!		sunshine winkles shells salty breezes suntan sand castles funfair sandy beaches

GUITAR	STAR	VINEGAR
	STAR IN STAR STAR IN STAR THE NIGHT STAR SHINING STAR BRIGHT STAR STAR	sour bitter pungent flavour sharp tang aroma

Difficult Poetry Snap

BAZAAR	CALENDAR	FAR
	January: Happy New Year February: Snowmen are here March: Mad as a hatter April: But it doesn't matter May: Don't cast a clout June: Till May is out July: Holidays are near August: Wish you were here September: School has begun October: Conkers for fun November: Skyrockets flew December: Merry Christmas to you.	remote misty infinite galaxy quasar unknown distant mysterious
I	**FLY**	**SLY**
me see hear touch taste smell talk listen		Sly mongoose Dog know you ways Sly mongoose Dog know you ways Mongoose went to de master's kitchen Pick up one of de fattest chicken Put it in de waistcoat pocket Sly mongoose!
SKY	**HORRIFY**	**BUTTERFLY**
Haiku Evening's ornament, The golden medallion Of the setting sun. *Chio*	fear awe trembling shivers down the spine nightmare terror macabre dread	

POETRY ADVENTURE

An ancient legend says that in the crypt of the local church is hidden a long lost poem by the famous writer William Shakespeare. It is worth a fortune if you find it, but also it is believed to contain the secret to his success. Just think, if you find it, you could be rich and famous! Why not try your luck to solve the poetic clues?

CARD 1. ENTERING THE CRYPT.

Legend says that the crypt can only be entered through the tomb of Sir Roger De Flambeaux. Examine it carefully. It is a typical medieval tomb, but there is no door. On the tomb is this poem which may contain a clue:

People who trouble to
Read these verses through
Even though they're hard
Should find the clue.

So study them with care
Then perhaps you'll know
How to move the stone
Enter, and walk below.

Even if you succeed
You must take care.
Evil awaits you
So beware!

SIR ROGER DE FLAMBEAUX

HOW WOULD YOU ENTER THE CRYPT?
When you have solved the clue, move on to Card 2.

CARD 2: THE STAIRWAY DOOR.

The tomb slides open revealing a staircase, down which you walk nervously. At the bottom of the stairs is a door with no handle. Instead there is a riddle to solve.

The world is upside down for me.
Night is my day.
I see through my ears.
But I find my way.
I can even fly.
What am I?

When you have solved the riddle, the door will open and you can move on to Card 3.

This page may be photocopied for classroom use only

CARD 3: THE CHAMBER DOOR.

The stairway door opens on to a long passageway. At the end of the passage is another door with this message written on it:

KNOCK AND ENTER.

You must knock the number of syllables in each line of this poem:

Grave guest
Haunting my house
On moonlit nights,
Spare me thy spectral glare -
Torment me no longer!

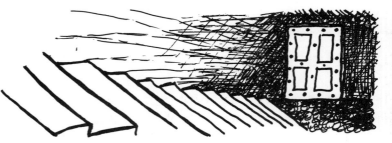

Check the numbers you have knocked and if you are right the door will open.
Go on to Card 4.

CARD 4: THE TOMBSTONES.

When you finally enter the chamber you find two tombstones. The treasure you are seeking is underneath one of them - but choose carefully! Something horrible lurks under the wrong one.

BENE
ATHTH ISST
ONE
A VAMPIRE LIE
SY OUW
I
LLL
EAV EH IM
HERE
I
FY O UAR
E WISE

THE
RE IS NOT
FARTOG
OYO URT
REA SU REL
I
ESBE LOW

Which stone will you choose? If you choose the right one, you have found the poem. Well done! If you choose the wrong one - you'd better run for it!

A video is often used to promote a pop song - why not try the same with poetry?
Instead of a budget of thousands of pounds, you will only have this sheet!

Part of the following poem has been turned into a video storyboard.

"No more the vampire nightly reaps
His bloody harvest." Sick with fear
The old man warns them but they sneer.
"He'll come again one day," he weeps,

"Among the graves, under those heaps
Of stone he waits - one day you'll jeer
no more!"

And outside as the darkness creeps
Over the church and graveyard drear,
A hand is groping from the bier,
It opens, and the vampire sleeps
No more.

Description of shot: Graveyard - night,
full moon, bat flying, gravestones.
Words from poem: _____

Music/sounds: Spooky organ music,
the hoot of an owl.

Description of shot: Scene in pub - old
man warns of vampire - zoom in on faces -
Words from poem: laughing.
"He'll come again one day."
Music/sounds: background music from
juke-box - chatter, clinking
of glasses.

Description of shot: Close-up - vampire's
grave - mysterious light - movement of
Words from poem: soil.
"Under those heaps / of stone he waits."
Music/sounds: Organ music - getting
louder - more atmospheric.

NOW ●Complete the storyboard, and add more verses to the poem describing what
the vampire does when he rises from his grave. Produce the storyboard to go
with it.

MAKE A POETRY VIDEO

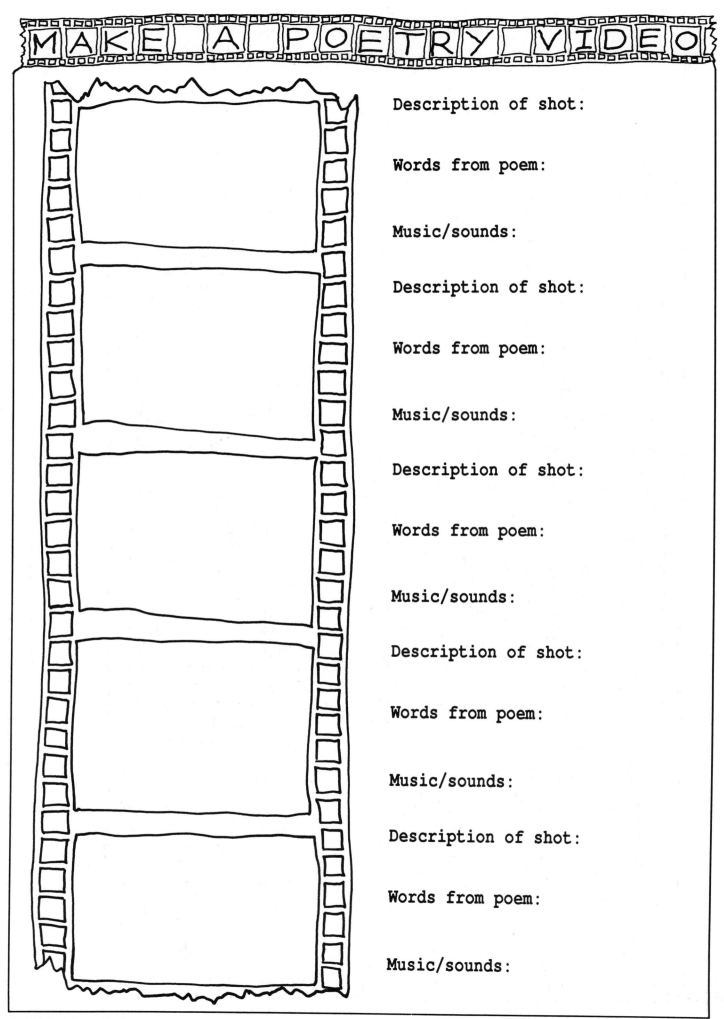

Description of shot:

Words from poem:

Music/sounds:

Description of shot:

Words from poem:

Music/sounds:

Description of shot:

Words from poem:

Music/sounds:

Description of shot:

Words from poem:

Music/sounds:

Description of shot:

Words from poem:

Music/sounds:

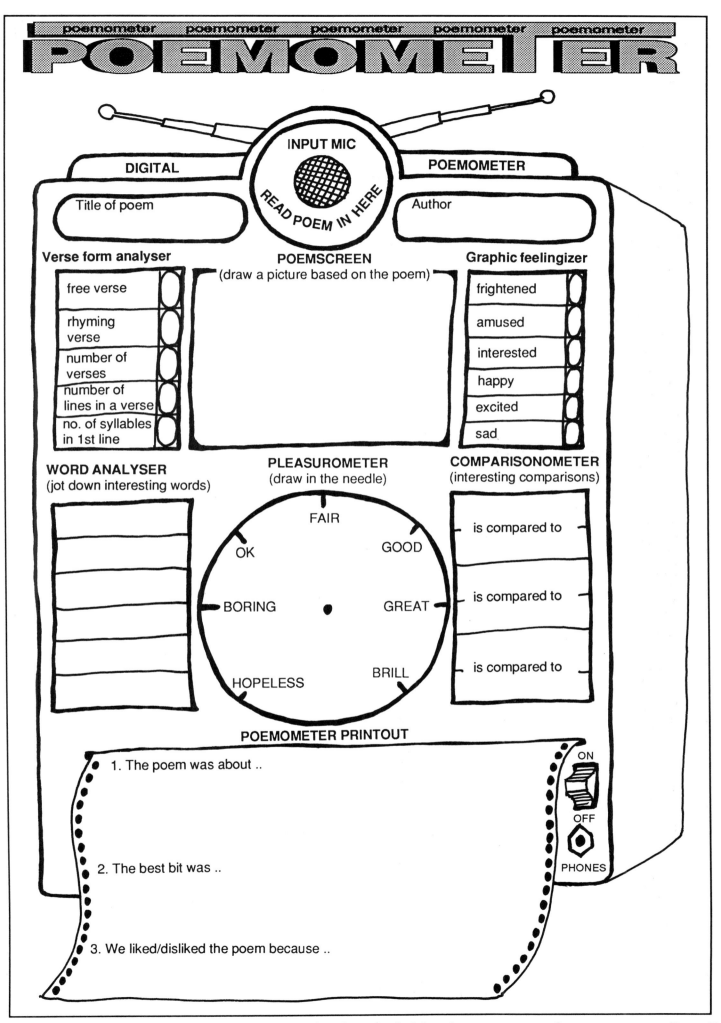

This page may be photocopied for classroom use only

Resource sheet - Poemometer.

Old Mrs Lazibones

Old Mrs Lazibones
And her dirty daughter
Never used soap
And never used water.
     Higgledy piggledy cowpat
     What d'you think of that?

Daisies from their fingernails,
Birds' nests in their hair-O,
Dandelions from their ears, -
What a dirty pair-O!
     Higgledy piggledy cowpat
     What d'you think of that?

Came a prince who sought a bride,
Riding past their doorstep,
Quick, said Mrs Lazibones.
Girl, under the watertap.
     Higgledy piggledy cowpat
     What d'you think of that?

Washed her up and washed her down,
Then she washed her sideways,
But the prince was far, far away,
He'd ridden off on highways.
     Higgledy piggledy cowpat
     What d'you think of that?

Gerda Mayer

Tyger! Tyger! burning bright
In the forests of the night,
What immortal hand or eye
Could frame thy fearful symmetry?

In what distant deeps or skies
Burnt the fire of thine eyes?
On what wings dare he aspire?
What the hand dare seize the fire?

And what shoulder, and what art,
Could twist the sinews of thy heart?
And when thy heart began to beat,
What dread hand and what dread feet?

What the hammer? What the chain?
In what furnace was thy brain?
What the anvil? What dread grasp
Dare its deadly terrors clasp?

When the stars threw down their spears,
And water'd heaven with their tears,
Did he smile his work to see?
Did he who made the Lamb make thee?

Tyger! Tyger! burning bright
In the forests of the night,
What immortal hand or eye,
Dare frame thy fearful symmetry?

William Blake

Jabberwocky

Twas brillig, and the slithy toves
Did gyre and gimble in the wabe;
All mimsy were the borogroves,
And the mome raths outgrabe.

"Beware the Jabberwock, my son!
The jaws that bite, the claws that catch!
Beware the Jubjub bird, and shun
The frumious Bandersnatch!"

He took his vorpal sword in hand:
Long time the manxome foe he sought -
So rested he by the Tumtum tree,
And stood awhile in thought.

And as in uffish thought he stood,
The Jabberwock, with eyes of flame,
Came whiffling through the tulgey wood,
And burbled as it came!

One, two! One, two! And through and through
The vorpal blade went snicker-snack!
He left it dead, and with its head
He went galumphing back.

"And hast thou slain the Jabberwock!
Come to my arms, my beamish boy!
O frabjous day! Callooh! Callay!"
He chortled in his joy.

'Twas brillig, and the slithy toves
Did gyre and gimble in the wabe;
All mimsy were the borrogroves,
And the mome raths outgrabe.

Lewis Carroll

Teachers' Notes

Page 7: Nursery Rhymes.
A resource sheet of other nursery rhymes has been provided. Many children do not know the "traditional" rhymes, so this is a useful exercise. Try collecting rhymes from any other cultures represented in the class. The rhymes have been selected for use with other topic work - number and counting, the months of the year, days of the week etc., as well as providing some strong imagery for art/design work. A more "modern" aspect of this kind of verse can be found in Gerda Mayer's work on page 42.

Pages 11 and 12: Simple Poetry Snap.
This is a game designed for two to four players. Pupils begin by cutting out the cards, shuffling and dealing. Play as ordinary snap, except that SNAP! is called when a rhyme is spotted. The winner of that round does not take all the accumulated cards, but ONLY the rhyming pair which are put to one side. Keep playing until all the cards are used up. Finally the pupils will have to make up poems using their words. Since the "snap" process will have produced rhyming words, they should find it easy to write a rhyming poem. The cards are also useful for building up spelling patterns. Photocopy them on to coloured paper to make them more attractive.

Pages 15 and 16: Three Poetry Formats.
Children often need help to structure their ideas. These three formats can help them to do that. The first two should help them to write list poems based on times of the day and days of the week. The third - the word-processor - is a little more complicated. A pair of pupils agree on a subject which they write in the appropriate box. Then they write as many words for that subject as they can think of in columns (a) and (b). By comparing notes and joint brainstorming, they fill in columns (c) and (d). The longer boxes can be used to jot down longer words and phrases, and the "scratchpad" for notes. Finally they can write their poem - either a joint or an individual effort - on the computer screen.

Page 17: Newspaper Poems.
This is an enjoyable activity because of the cutting and sticking involved. Pupils, working in pairs, choose a subject and look through old newspapers (preferably pruned of unsuitable material, pin-ups, etc.) for suitable headlines. Finally, they sort their headlines into an order which "telegraphs" a message. The best results are achieved if you prevent pupils from just assembling material into continuous prose, e.g. by limiting it to a word or phrase per line. All this is best explained to pupils using the example provided.

Page 21: Riddles.
These introduce other writing systems and secret alphabets as a way of disguising riddles. This is great fun as well as providing insight into writing systems and improving hand-eye coordination.
ANSWERS: RAKE, BOW.

Pages 25 and 26: Computapoem.
These sheets need to be cut out and assembled very carefully for the best results. Work on parts of speech will be central to this activity, and it could be linked with the computer shape on Page 16. A valuable follow-up would be to read some of Edwin Morgan's poetry, e.g. "The Computer's first Christmas Card".

Pages 30 and 31: Accent and Dialect.
Accent and dialect are important aspects of knowledge about language. Poems on these sheets need to be read aloud in a good imitation of the appropriate accent/dialect.

Pages 32 and 33: Free Verse.
Free verse can be one of the hardest kinds of poetry for young people to write. Simply, there is too much freedom and they do not know what to do. The structured activities here will help pupils to understand how best to lay out free verse. The original version on page 33 should be given to compare the children's own versions, but it is important to stress that other alternatives could be just as good. Note that the two free verse poems in this unit follow the convention of beginning lines with a capital letter. It should be pointed out that this is optional.

Page 36: The Worst Poet in the World.
"The Frog and the Princess" was written by William Worthless. Other authors are as follows: "The Wild Hog" - a traditional ballad; "Windy Nights" - R. L. Stevenson; "The Eagle" - Tennyson.
The important thing about this exercise is the discussion about what makes a "good" poem. Pupils' ideas about this can be consolidated into a Poetry Competition, and by compiling a poetry "top ten", (see page 6).

Pages 37 and 38: Difficult Poetry Snap.

This is a more sophisticated version of the earlier Poetry Snap game. The following instructions can be read out or photocopied:

1. Play in pairs.
2. Cut out the cards, shuffle them and divide them between you.
3. Play the game like ordinary snap - shout SNAP! when you see a RHYMING HEADWORD.
4. Pick up and put to one side the pair of rhyming cards only.
5. Continue re-using the cards until they are all (or nearly all) gone.
6. Now look at the cards you have laid aside. The player who did best at SNAP will have the greatest variety - but is not the winner - yet!
7. Use the pictures, poems, words and rhymes to inspire you to write your own poems. The person who writes the best poem wins! This should be decided by discussion and not by voting alone.
8. The game works better and is more enjoyable if you add more sets of cards following the same pattern. Work in pairs to design your own.

Pages 39 and 40: Poetry Adventure.

This adventure game depends on a knowledge of acrostics, riddles, syllables and codes and will work best for pupils who have covered these topics - see pages 18, 20, 21. The most fruitful aspect of this activity is the follow-up, when pupils can design their own poetry adventure.
ANSWERS: Card 1 - an acrostic, PRESS THE EYES. Card 2 - a riddle, a BAT. Card 3 - the number of syllables is 2, 4, 4, 6, 6. Card 4 - the first tombstone reads BENEATH THIS STONE A VAMPIRE LIES / YOU'LL LEAVE HIM HERE IF YOU ARE WISE, and the second reads THERE IS NOT FAR TO GO / YOUR TREASURE LIES BELOW.

Page 41: Make a Poetry Video.

This idea can provide an exciting and rewarding way for pupils to explore a poem. The success of the activity depends on choosing the right poem for the group concerned. A good way to follow up this preparatory material would be to use a book like "Nightmares: Poems to Trouble Your Sleep" by Jack Prelutsky (A & C Black). A resource sheet on page 42 is provided for photocopying.

Page 43: Poemometer.

Close analysis of poetry need not wait until the secondary school. The Poemometer provides a "fun" way of making a start in this direction. Use it alongside your existing classroom anthologies, or use the resource poems provided on page 44. You could enlarge the Poemometer to A3 on your copier to provide more space for writing.

HOW TO USE THE POEMOMETER.

1. Explain to the group that the real Poetometer will give an instant report on any poem that is read into it, but unfortunately the worksheet version has to be done by hand!
2. In pairs, pupils read their poem into the "input mic.", sharing the reading in any way they think appropriate.
3. Pupils discuss the poem and fill in the readout boxes as appropriate.
4. Some of the terms used may need to be explained, but all are covered by the sheets in this book. Do not let the format of the Poemometer dominate your teaching - blank out any terms which you feel unsuitable. The "verse-form analyser" is a good example of this. Syllables and beats may be counted out by clapping etc., but if both concepts are new to them, it would be confusing to introduce them both together.
5. Help pupils to fill in the Poemometer by giving them an example. If you use a simile such as "The snow covered our village like a white, woolly blanket", then on the COMPARISONOMETER, you would write, "snow" being compared to "a white woolly blanket".
6. It may not be appropriate to use sophisticated terms like "simile", but this device enables you to lay the simple foundations and leave the terms until later.
7. The Poemometer works particularly well when used with a specified set of poems or anthology. Completed Poemometers can then be displayed so that pupils can follow each other's recommendations.

Follow all this up by comparing Poemometers dealing with the same poem, or even use the words in the "word analyser" as the basis for a poem.

Page 47: Become a Poet Board Game.

Pupils will need to have covered many of the activities in this book to solve the problems in the game, and so it is a kind of assessment. The game works without dice - the initial rhyme quiz in the start box ensures that players will start at different places on the board.
As a final touch, you could award pupils a POETIC LICENCE, perhaps getting them to design it themselves, and not forgetting to explain what POETIC LICENSE is!

Become a poet board game

For 2 to 4 players. No dice needed. Cut out the counters.

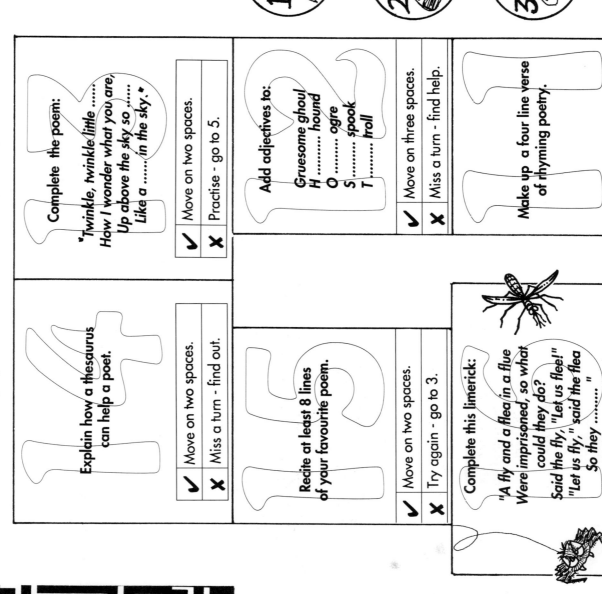

START

Give as many rhymes as you can for:

PLAYER 1 : print
PLAYER 2 : love
PLAYER 3 : flame
PLAYER 4 : crab

Move on the number of rhymes you thought of.

1

How many syllables in "grasshopper"?

✔ Move on one space.
✘ Try again next turn.

2

Give three rhymes for "ghost".

✔ Move on one space.

3

Complete the poem:

"Twinkle, twinkle little ......
How I wonder what you are,
Up above the sky so ......
Like a ...... in the sky."

✔ Move on two spaces.
✘ Practise - go to 5.

4

Explain how a thesaurus can help a poet.

✔ Move on two spaces.
✘ Miss a turn - find out.

5

Recite at least 8 lines of your favourite poem.

✔ Move on two spaces.
✘ Try again - go to 3.

6

Complete this limerick:

"A fly and a flea in a flue
Were imprisoned, so what could they do?
Said the fly, "Let us flee!"
"Let us fly," said the flea
So they .... "

✔ Move on one space.

7

Add adjectives to:

Gruesome ghoul
H .... hound
O .... ogre
S .... spook
T .... troll

✔ Move on three spaces.
✘ Miss a turn - find help.

8

Make up a four line verse of rhyming poetry.

✔ Move on three spaces.

1
2
3
4

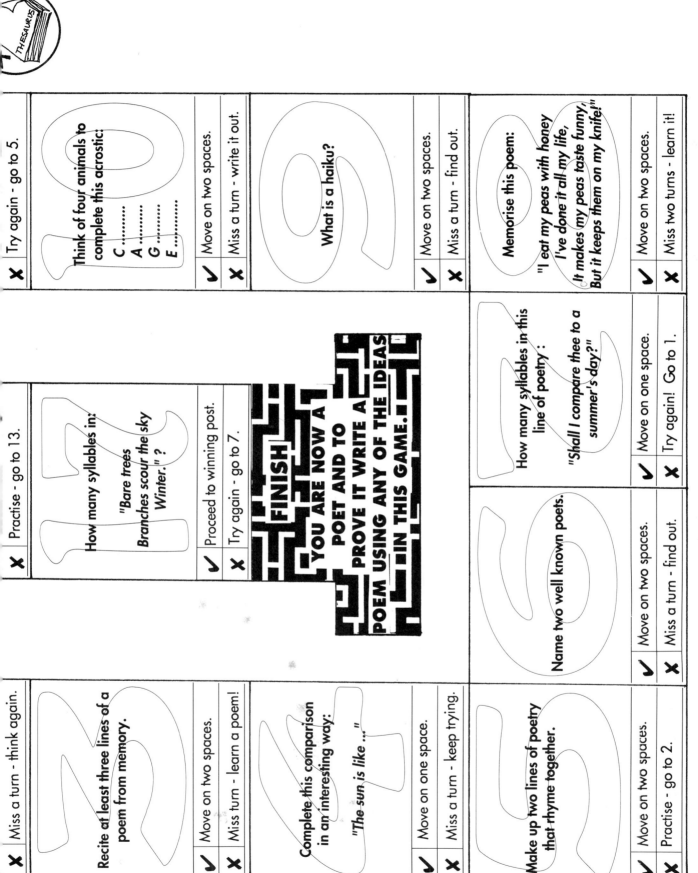

X Try again - go to 5.

Think of four animals to complete this acrostic:

C ....
A ....
G ....
E ....

✔ Move on two spaces.
X Miss a turn - write it out.

What is a haiku?

✔ Move on two spaces.
X Miss a turn - find out.

Memorise this poem:

"I eat my peas with honey
I've done it all my life,
It makes my peas taste funny,
But it keeps them on my knife!"

✔ Move on two spaces.
X Miss two turns - learn it!

X Practise - go to 13.

How many syllables in:

"Bare trees
Branches scour the sky
Winter." ?

✔ Proceed to winning post.
X Try again - go to 7.

FINISH

YOU ARE NOW A POET AND TO PROVE IT WRITE A POEM USING ANY OF THE IDEAS IN THIS GAME.

How many syllables in this line of poetry :

"Shall I compare thee to a summer's day?"

✔ Move on one space.
X Try again! Go to 1.

Name two well known poets.

✔ Move on two spaces.
X Miss a turn - find out.

X Miss a turn - think again.

Recite at least three lines of a poem from memory.

✔ Move on two spaces.
X Miss turn - learn a poem!

Complete this comparison in an interesting way:

"The sun is like ..."

✔ Move on one space.
X Miss a turn - keep trying.

Make up two lines of poetry that rhyme together.

✔ Move on two spaces.
X Practise - go to 2.

Further Information

Useful sources of material:

Dragon in the Woodshed, SCHOLARSTOWN
Digging for China, SCHOLARSTOWN
Exploring Poetry 5-8, Balaam and Merrick, NATE
Poems for 7 years Old and Under, Helen Nicholl, PUFFIN
Please Mrs Butler, Allan Ahlberg, PUFFIN
Standing on a Strawberry, John Cunliffe, DEUTSCH
Diddle, diddle, dumpling, Tomie De Paola, MAGNET
Meet My Folks, Ted Hughes, FABER
Jelly Pie (Cassette), Roger McGough and Brian Pattern, PUFFIN
Rhyme Time, ed. Barbara Ireson, BEAVER
Salford Road, Gareth Owen, KESTREL
Don't Put the Mustard in the Custard, Rosen and Blake, DEUTSCH
Warning: Too Much Schooling Can Damage Your Health, Millum, E J ARNOLD
School's Out!, John Foster, OXFORD
Poetry Through Humour and Horror, Chris Webster, CASSELL
Press for Action Poetry, Gould and Tunstall, FOLENS
You'll Love this Stuff! Poems from Many Cultures, Morag Styles, CAMBRIDGE
The Poetry Processor, Paul Higgins, BLACKWELL
I See a Voice, Michael Rosen, HUTCHINSON
You Tell Me, Michael Rosen and Roger McGough, PUFFIN
Song of the City, Gareth Owen, FONTANA LION
Caribbean Anthology, ILEA Learning Materials Service
In the Glassroom, Roger McGough, CAPE

Useful reference material:

NATEPACK One: Poetry. Available from NATE
Not "Daffodils Again!". Teaching Poetry 9-13, Longman Resouces Unit
A Poet's Manual and Rhyming Dictionary, Frances Stillman, THAMES and HUDSON
To Speak True: The Art of Speaking Poetry, Betty Mulcahy, PERGAMON
Does It Have to Rhyme? and *What Rhymes with Secret?*, Sandy Brownjohn, HODDER
Poetry Experience, Stephen Tunnicliffe, METHUEN
A Linguistic Guide to English Poetry, Geoffrey Leech, LONGMAN
Dictionary and Handbook of Poetry, Myers and Simms, LONGMAN
Poetry in the Making, Ted Hughes, FABER

Useful addresses:

The Schools' Poetry Association. 27 Pennington Close, Colden Common, Winchester, Hants SO21 1UR Tel: 0962 712062

The Poetry Society. 21 Earls Court Square, London SW5 9DE
Tel: 071 373 7861

The Arts Council Poetry Library. The South Bank Centre, Royal Festival Hall, London SE1 8XX Tel: 071 921 0943